Personal Bible Study:
A How-To

Personal Bible Study: A How-To

by
RUTH SUN

MOODY PRESS
CHICAGO

ISBN: 0-8024-4574-8

Printed in the United States of America

To those who are in the
Discipleship Training Program

CONTENTS

1

STUDY THE BIBLE WITH HEART AND MIND

The two-fold nature of the Scripture—divine and human—makes it of paramount importance to study the Bible with both heart and mind.

It is a fundamental belief of Christians that the Bible is a unique book, and its uniqueness lies in the fact that it is a product of double authorship—the Divine and the human.

First, the Bible had its origin in God, who took the initiative to reveal Himself to mankind. Second, in revealing Himself, God communicated through men, and chose human language as the vehicle. Biblical authors spoke from God, not from their own impulse but as they were moved by the Holy Spirit (2 Peter 1:21).

Therefore, it logically follows that our approach and study method must be consistent with that two-fold nature of the Bible. Since it is the revelation of God, we must study it like no other book, following *the law of the Spirit.* Also, since it is written in human language, we must study it like every other book, observing the *laws of language.* Above all, it is of paramount importance that we study the Bible with both *heart* and *mind:* an obedient heart and an active mind.

THE LAW OF THE SPIRIT

The divine origin of the Scriptures makes the illumination of the Holy Spirit indispensable in Bible study.

Since the Bible is the Word of God, divine illumination is essential to an understanding of the Word. The Bible makes it clear that in order to receive that illumination one must be *born of the Spirit.* That is, we must have the Holy Spirit within us (1 Corinthians 2:11-16). Without this indwelling we have no capacity to receive the ministry of the Spirit. Second, we must have a *babe-like attitude* totally dependent on the Holy Spirit (Matthew 11:25-26). For those reasons, Bible study should at least include the following steps.

BEGIN WITH PRAYER

"Open my eyes, that I may behold wondrous things out of Thy law" (Psalm 119:18).

The most important step in Bible study is to pray before studying. We should ask the Spirit to teach (John 14:26), to guide (John 16:12), and to illuminate our study so that the veil may be removed

(2 Corinthians 3:16), so that we may come to see and to perceive the truth. Remember, the Word of God is spiritual and must be spiritually discerned.

Although the importance of prayer in Bible study cannot be overemphasized, the importance of having a right attitude is something that should not be ignored. In truth, our attitude will determine whether or not the Bible study is profitable. A fruitful Bible study must be accompanied with:

A teachable heart—a readiness to learn. A heart prepared to receive illumination and instructions. A heart ready to say, "Speak, LORD, for Thy servant is listening" (1 Samuel 3:9).

A sincere anticipation—a humble expectancy. It is an expectation to hear God speaking to us through what we study, believing that God rewards those who seek Him (Hebrews 11:6).

PROCEED WITH MEDITATION

"Make me understand . . . so I will meditate on Thy wonders" (Psalm 119:27).

According to Webster, to meditate is "to think deeply and continuously; to reflect; to ponder." Let us make no mistake. To rely on the Spirit is no substitute for thinking, nor is it an excuse for laziness, and certainly it does not mean a passive attitude. Obviously, that was the mistake of the Corinthian church. They were rich in spiritual gifts (1:7), yet they lacked in knowledge and understanding (3:16; 5:6; 6:2-3, 9, 15-16, 19; 10:1; 12:1); they had the manifestation of the working of the Spirit (12:14), yet they failed to exercise their minds (10:15; 11:13).

We must not neglect the fact that God expects us to use the mind He has given us and to use it diligently. The commands such as, "Consider what I say" (2 Timothy 2:7), or "you judge what I say" (1 Corinthians 10:15; Luke 12:57) definitely appeal to human reasoning. So, understanding God's Word actually requires more than the ministry of the Spirit; it also requires an open and active mind.

An open mind. Without it learning will be impossible. We must be open to the Spirit for correction as well as instruction. It is necessary to bear in mind that we must guard against the error of using the Bible as proof text to support our preconceived ideas. Rather, we must bring those ideas under the scrutiny of the Word of God.

An inquisitive mind. An active, inquisitive mind is essential for effective Bible study, for it enables us to get to the heart of the text. Always remember, illumination of the Spirit is enhanced rather than inhibited by an active, inquisitive mind.

CONCLUDE WITH PERSONAL APPLICATION

"Give me understanding, that I may observe Thy law, and keep it with all my heart" (Psalm 119:34).

The ultimate end of Bible study is not only to gain factual information, though that is basic. The ultimate aim of Bible study is to bring the newly discovered truth to bear upon our lives. Fruitfulness in Bible study depends not only on *how* we study, but also on *what* response we make to its message. An effective Bible study requires a surrendered will and an obedient heart.

A surrendered will. A will resolved to do His will is a fundamental condition of profitable Bible study (John 7:17).

An obedient heart. When the *mind* comes to understand the message, the *heart* must respond, and the *will* must act upon it. Response comes the moment we apply the message to our life situation. By the act of obedience we become doers of the Word and not hearers only (James 1:22), and our obedience is the proof of our love for Christ (John 14:15).

So we must pray that the same Spirit who *enlightens* us will both *enable* us to obey the light, and *empower* us to translate the message into our daily life.

THE LAWS OF LANGUAGE

The human authorship of the Bible makes it mandatory that the laws of language be followed in interpreting the Bible.

In one sense the Bible is like other literature, a product of men, but it was a product of men under providential guidance. If it is literature written in ordinary language, then we must study it as we would any other book, observing the common rules of language in order to grasp accurately its meaning. In other words, if we want to know what the biblical authors really said, it is imperative that we study their writings properly. Without question that takes time and effort.

It is well to remember that our dependency on the illumination of the Spirit is not incompatible with the effort on our part to understand the Bible. On the contrary, the divine illumination and human effort must go hand in hand if we are to accurately understand its message.

Paul wrote to young Timothy, *"Be diligent* to present yourself approved to God as a workman who does not need to be ashamed, *handling accurately* the word of truth" (2 Timothy 2:15, italics added). Timothy must make every effort ("be diligent" is imperative in Greek) to handle rightly the Word of God ("handling accurately"—the Greek word means "to cut straight"; thus, "to guide the Word of God along a straight line"), so that he may win God's approval as a workman, and have no reason for shame before his Master. The same diligence required of Timothy is also required of us today. The Word of God must be handled correctly. Here are some essential rules that will help us in that regard.

OBSERVE THE CONTEXT

We must interpret a given text (whether a word, a sentence, a paragraph, or a passage) in the light of its context.

A context is what goes before and after a text. The importance of context cannot be overemphasized, since thought is usually expressed in a series of related ideas. Many would agree that neglect of the context is a common cause of erroneous interpretation and irrelevant application. It becomes obvious that our responsibility is to study the context first, observing the train of thought, and then to interpret the text in that light.

Some helpful guidelines:

Always observe the context first. A careful study of the context often sheds light on the meaning of the text under study. As a rule, start with the immediate context, then the remote context, and finally the total context.

- Immediate context—what precedes and what follows.

- Remote context—If the immediate context gives no help, then we go to the remote context, the chapter or the book where the text under study is found.

- Total context—Again, if the remote context sheds no light, then we must interpret the text in the light of the total teaching of the Bible, the total context.

This procedure is based on the principle of harmony, that the revelation of God is self-consistent.

Get acquainted with the outline of the book in which the text is found. It enables us not only to discover the context of the text, but also to see the objective the author had in mind in composing that particular portion of materials.

Pay attention to the connectives. The connectives may seem insignificant, yet they often reveal the development of thoughts and how verses, paragraphs, and passages are related to each other. As a rule, a connective connects a thought with the one immediately before it, though there are exceptions to the rule. In the gospels we may find passages grouped together without connectives. In such cases, we must not always assume that they are not related. Some, indeed, are not logically related to one another, but others are clearly related in spite of the absence of the connectives.

Study parallel passages carefully. Study of the parallel passages may prove to be helpful in determining the context and the meaning of the text as well.

STUDY THE BACKGROUND

We must interpret the text in the light of its original historical-cultural setting.

We must remember that the Bible was originally written to a particular people of a particular age in a particular land, and often to meet a particular need. To be more precise, the Bible was written originally to Jews (the Old Testament) and Gentile Christians (the New Testament) of the first century A.D. or much earlier in Palestine and its surrounding countries. Therefore, it is no surprise that the Bible reflects a culture unfamiliar to us. For that reason, we must study the world of biblical authors in order to interpret their writings correctly. Knowledge of customs, culture, geography, religion, and the life situation of the first century and Old Testament times is not only helpful, but also essential. A word of caution! We must carefully guard against the error of interpreting the text against the twentieth century life setting.

Two sources of information are helpful.

Internal. The Bible is the principal source of essential background information. Here are some practical suggestions:

1. Read the Bible. The more we are familiar with the Bible, the more background knowledge we gain.

2. Take notes. Systematically file the acquired information. It will prove to be very useful later.

External. Bible dictionaries, good commentaries, and Bible handbooks are very helpful sources of information in external background study.

UNDERSTAND THE WORDS

We must interpret the words according to the sense in which the author used them.

Words are important because they are the basic unit of meaning. Thus, by understanding the words, we understand the Bible. In general, each word has several meanings. But under normal circumstance, in a given situation, that word has only one meaning, whether literal or figurative. Therefore, our responsibility would be to discover the sense in which the author used a particular word.

Some helpful guidelines:

Recognize the literary type. First, recognize the literary form of the passage (or the book), because it determines the frame of reference in which the word is used. There are a variety of literary types found in the Bible, such as prose narrative, poetry, parabolic literature, and apocalyptic literature.

Look for the natural sense. Always look for the natural and obvious meaning. Keep in mind that the natural meaning is not necessarily always the literal meaning. Sometimes, it is figurative. As a rule, follow the literal meaning unless it makes no sense and leads to absurdity.

Observe the context. Determine the meaning of a word by the context in which it occurs. As a rule, a given word usually has the same meaning in all of its occurrences in a single passage. Yet the same word may have different meanings in different passages. In one case it may be used in a literal sense, and in another passage in a figurative sense. Again, the context will provide the answer.

Study words. Studying the given word and its synonyms in other passages enables us to determine the meaning. An unabridged English dictionary, a Bible dictionary, a good concordance, and a reference Bible are invaluable tools for studying the words.

Study the figures of speech. A figure of speech is an expression that uses words in a "nonliteral" sense to give vividness and to arrest the attention of hearers. Examples include similes, metaphors, and personification. Since the Bible abounds in figurative language, it is important that we study biblical hermeneutics and learn the principles that govern the interpretation of the figurative expression employed.

EZRA, OUR MODEL

"For Ezra had set his heart
to study the law of the LORD,
and to practice it,
and to teach his statutes and ordinances in Israel" (Ezra 7:10).

"Ezra had set his heart"	DETERMINATION	Inward preparation
	Concern with *preparation* • Where is the Word of God in my priorities?	
"To study"	OBSERVATION	Objective study
	Concern with *facts* • What does the author actually write?	
	INTERPRETATION	
	Concern with *meaning* • What does the author mean?	
"To practice"	APPLICATION	Subjective experience
	Concern with *practice* • What does it mean to me here and now? • How does it touch my life?	
"To teach"	COMMUNICATION	Outward expression
	Concern with *method* • How do I share? • How do I lead a Bible study?	

2

EZRA, OUR MODEL

DETERMINATION

"For Ezra *had set his heart* . . ." (Ezra 7:10, italics added).

To "set one's heart" implies a preparation of heart before the preparation of mind, an essential step in studying the Word of God. To "set" also has the idea of arranging things in priority according to their value. Ezra was convinced that the study of the Word of God should be on the top of his priority list. He was sure of it! We should also have the same conviction and make the study of the Word the object of our hearts' desires.

Let us remember that it is impossible to truly love God and neglect His Word. As Derek Prince well points out:

> Your attitude toward God's Word is your attitude toward God Himself. You do not love God more than you love His Word. You do not obey God more than you obey His Word. You do not honor God more than you honor His Word. You do not have more room in your heart and life for God than you

have for His Word. Do you want to know how much God means to you? You can easily find out. Just ask yourself, How much does God's Word mean to me? The answer to the second question is the answer also to the first. God means as much to you as His Word means to you—just that much, and no more.[1]

Suggestions:

1. *Take an inventory.* First take an inventory of your life. As honestly as you can, answer this question: "Where is the study of the Word of God in my priorities?"

2. *Make the decisions.* Time often is the number one enemy in studying the Word of God. Remember, you will never find the time; you will have to take the time. Before you venture into this project make these decisions.

   • Determine the amount of time you can spend studying God's Word each day.

   • Determine the best time of the day for studying God's Word. Choose a time when you are fresh in body, mind, and spirit. If possible, make it the same time every day.

OBSERVATION

"Ezra had set his heart *to study* . . ." (Ezra 7:10, italics added).

Ezra had set his heart to study the Word of God. To

be sure, studying requires time and concentration. Studying the Word involves two steps, *observation* and *interpretation*. Observe this order always! Interpretation must be based on observation.

Observation is a careful searching for facts with the intent to find out what the author actually says. That requires more than just physical sight, it requires a mental awareness of what we see and read.

In observing an *action* (or a narrative) passage, ask basic questions, such as:

- *Who?*—people, identity
- *What?*—event, reaction, result
- *When?*—time, date, season
- *Where?*—geographical location
- *Why?*—cause, reason
- *How?*—method

In observing a *thought* (or logical) passage, take notice of:

- *Literary form*—poetry? prose? dialogue?
- *Words and phrases*—key words or phrases? recurring words? unfamiliar words?
- *Expression*—idiomatic expression? figures of speech?
- *Grammar*—verb? noun? pronoun? conjunction? command? question?

- *Structure of paragraphs*—how are they related to each other? to the chapter? Are there contrasts? comparisons?

Insignificant as they might appear, these questions enable us to see things as they really are. They are also keys to the mastery of the content. Remember, correct interpretation depends upon accurate observation.

Suggestions:

1. Read the passage over and over again. Don't assume you have seen everything in the passage with the first reading. If you would read it over carefully, you may be surprised to find how little you saw before.

2. Use pencil and paper. Make it a habit to study the Bible with pen in hand. Systematically record your observations as you read. This will enable you: 1) to grasp what you read, 2) to see the structure of the passage, and 3) to notice the train of thought.

INTERPRETATION

Whenever there is communication, verbal or written, there is interpretation whether or not we are aware of it. We are not aware of the presence of interpretation when the material is familiar to us because it takes place spontaneously. But it becomes obvious in the case of difficult material, such as the literary work of the past, because the process of our understanding has been broken. Frequently, a gap seems to develop between the material and us—a distance between the author and reader. Therefore, interpretation is needed to bridge the gap or remove the distance, thus making the strange material understandable.

Interpretation involves an effort to discover the intended meaning of the author. That is done with the help of some guidelines. To determine what the author meant when the passage was written, two basic questions must be raised:

1. What did the author mean by this word, phrase, or clause?

   How did his first readers understand it?

2. What does this word, phrase, or clause imply?

Make sure we do not read twentieth-century ideas into the text and make the author say what he did not intend to say. The best way to avoid misunderstanding the author is to project ourselves back into the author's day. Try to put yourself in his shoes and think his thoughts. Remember, relevant application depends on sound and correct interpretation.

Suggestions:

1. Study tools: an unabridged English dictionary, Bible dictionaries and commentaries, and a concordance are most helpful.

2. Word study.

    a. Get all the meanings listed in the dictionary, including the root meaning.

    b. Tentatively decide on the meaning that best fits this particular context.

    c. Check to see how the word is used in other passages, especially by the same author. Use a concordance.

    d. Determine the meaning of the word in the text under study. Consult good commentaries to make sure your interpretation is accurate.

APPLICATION

"For Ezra had set his heart to study . . . and *to practice* it" (Ezra 7:10, italics added).

Ezra did not study the Word simply for the sake of studying, but he studied it with a view to practice the truth. The book of Ezra, indeed, bears witness to that fact. By applying the law of the Lord, Ezra brought about the transformation of the national life of Israel, which resulted in unprecedented revival.

Let us keep in mind that the Bible was not written primarily for our information, but for our transformation. In writing to Timothy, the apostle Paul stated clearly the nature and the purpose of the Bible. He said, "The whole Bible was given to us by inspiration from God and useful to teach us what is true and to make us realize what is wrong in our lives; it straightens us out and helps us to do what is right . . ." (2 Timothy 3:16, TLB).* According to this verse, the four-fold purpose of the Bible is:

- *To teach us what is true.* So, as we read we ask ourselves, Is there any new light about God? Christ? the Holy Spirit? Satan?

- *To make us realize what is wrong in our lives.* Then ask, Is there a specific sin God wants me to confess and to forsake?

- *To straighten out our lives.* Then ask, Is there a good example God wants me to follow? Is there a bad example to avoid?

- *To help us do what is right.* Then ask, Is there a command I should obey? a promise I may claim?

The apostle James also reminds us, "And remember, it is a message to obey, not just to listen to, so don't fool yourself" (1:22, TLB). In other words, Bible study calls for action. Without application Bible study will be a meaningless activity. Therefore, we must take time to think through thoroughly the personal application. Ask yourself the following questions:

1. What biblical principle (s) do I find in this passage? (Principles may be stated explicitly or only implied in the text.)

The Living Bible.

2. How can I apply the newly found principle (s) to my daily life?

3. What change in my life must be made in the light of what I learned?

Suggestions:

Keep a notebook. Put down: 1) date, 2) Scripture references, 3) biblical principle (s) , 4) the decision or commitment you have made before the Lord. Be very specific! and 5) Keep a prayer record of God's answers to your prayers.

In short, "Apply yourself wholly to the Bible; apply the Bible wholly to yourself" (Bengel).

COMMUNICATION

"For Ezra had set his heart to study . . . and to practice . . . and to *teach*" (Ezra 7:10, italics added).

Consult chapter 5, "How to Lead a Group Bible Study-Discussion."

NOTE

1. Derek Prince, *Foundations for Faith*, Foundation Series: Book I (Ft. Lauderdale, Fla.: Derek Prince Publications, 1965-66), p. 20.

3

A SURVEY OF A BOOK

A survey of an entire book is necessary for the study of its individual passages. A passage can be fully understood only when it is seen in relation to the book as a whole. For that reason, the knowledge of the book as a whole is essential. Since a survey is a general comprehensive study of the book, you must not be bogged down by the details or sidetracked by difficult verses or passages. Always keep the *objective* before you. Make sure you have the following basic tools:

- Bible—use the New American Standard Bible or the New International Version.
- Pencil and paper—always take notes in your Bible study.
- English dictionary—be sure to look up any unfamiliar word in an unabridged dictionary.
- Bible dictionary—get a copy of a good Bible dictionary.

Be aware of the seven "B's" before you study the Bible:

1. Be alert!—don't study the Bible with a sleepy head.

2. Be attentive!—don't let the mind wander.

3. Be observant!—don't read aimlessly.

4. Be inquisitive!—don't be content with the obvious.

5. Be diligent!—don't spare any effort.

6. Be persistent!—don't quit.

7. Be honest!—don't fool yourself.

Observe the following steps as you survey a book.

GET ACQUAINTED WITH THE BOOK

Objective: To learn the general content of the book, its author, recipients, and purpose.

STUDYING THE GOSPELS

Read through the entire book at least four times during the week. Be sure to write down your observations and impressions and their references. Learn to organize your notes, charts, and other personal helps in a graphic way so that the information will be easily accessible.

First day. Find a block of time that will allow you to read the entire book at one sitting without interruption. Get the feel of the book.

Second and third days. Read through the book again. Jot down the characters and indicate their relation to Jesus. Always remember to put down the references.

Fourth and fifth days. Again read over the gospel. List the miracles including occasion, nature, purpose, and the reaction of the people. Also indicate what each miracle reveals about the person of Jesus.

Sixth and seventh days. Go over the book again. Make a separate list of parables and discourses with a sentence or two to summarize their purpose/message. Also, jot down your observation of Jesus as a teacher in each situation.

It will be helpful if you would jot down questions you would like to ask, topics you would like to pursue, and verses you would like to memorize on separate sheets of paper as you read the book.

STUDYING THE EPISTLES

Read the entire book at least once a day throughout the week. Again, put down your observations with the references on separate sheets of paper each day.

First day. Read the entire book at one sitting without break or interruption. Get the feel of the book.

Second day. Read through the book again. This time read more slowly and carefully. Jot down your observations and impressions concerning the author, such as:

• The name of the author

• The mood of the author as it is reflected in the book

• The whereabouts of the author at the time of writing

- The physical condition or the circumstance of the author

- The life and character of the author.

Third day. Go over the book again. This time jot down your observations and impressions concerning the recipients, such as:

- Who are the recipients?

- What is said about them implicitly and explicitly?

- Are there any indications as to their physical circumstances and spiritual condition?

- What was their pressing need? What difficulty did they experience?

Fourth day. Read the entire book over again, and note its purpose.

- Is the purpose of the book stated explicitly?

- Is there any indication as to why this book was written?

Fifth day. Read through the book again and jot down the time element, and record any geographical references. (If possible, locate those references on a map found in the back of your Bible.)

Sixth day. Read through the book once more. State in your own words:

- The central theme of the book

- The main teaching of the book

- The characteristics of the book.

DISCOVER THE AUTHOR'S BLUEPRINT

Objectives: To find out the structure or the outline of the book. To see how the author laid down his material, and how each part is related to one another and to the whole.

STRUCTURAL ANALYSIS

There are two ways of approach.

For shorter books such as epistles.

1. Look for major divisions.
    a. Go through the book again and notice the major breaks in the thought. Pay close attention to the connectives. In case of a historical book, take notice of the major events, characters, and geographical references.

    b. Give an appropriate title to each division. Make the title as precise a statement of the general contents of the division as possible.

2. Look for natural subdivisions.
    a. Go through the major divisions and find natural subdivisions. Again, take notice of connectives, comparisons, contrasts, and repetitions.

    b. Give a suitable title to each subdivision. If possible, make the titles of the subdivisions relate to the title of the division.

For longer books such as the gospels.

1. Begin with paragraphs.

    a. Read through the book paragraph by paragraph.

    b. Give a title to each paragraph. A title must be brief, just a word or a phrase.

2. Combine paragraphs into units.

    a. Go through the paragraphs and combine those that are logically related into a unit. Logical relation may be in terms of thought, event, or character.

    b. Give an appropriate title to each unit.

3. Combine units into sections, and sections into divisions.

    a. Following the procedure mentioned above, combine the related units into sections, and sections into divisions.

    b. Again, give a title to each section, and then to each division. The title should be precise and terse, yet one that well summarizes the general content of the section or division.

STRUCTURAL RELATIONSHIP

Draw an outline of the book. Review the structural analysis and work out an outline of the book.

Discover the structure of the book. Study the outline of the book until you see how each part is related to the other and to the whole and how the author unfolds his thought and accomplishes his goal.

CONSULT OUTSIDE AIDS

Objectives: To compare the results of your own study with those reached by others, and to obtain the background information that is difficult to gather from the book itself.

COMPARE THE RESULTS

When you have finished the first two steps, you should consult a good dictionary or commentary.

OBTAIN THE BACKGROUND INFORMATION

Read the introduction to the book under survey in a good Bible dictionary or commentary. Jot down information such as:

- Author
- Recipient
- Purpose
- Date and place of writing
- Characteristics of the book
- Outline of the book.

With the epistle, also take notice of:

- The origin of the church
- The historical, cultural, political, and religious background of the city in which the church is found
- The geographical location of the church and its significance.

4

A DETAILED STUDY OF A PASSAGE

Preliminary Consideration

A STUDY UNIT

A passage as a study unit should be a natural unit of thought or a compositional unit. The chapter divisions as you find them in the English translations do not always constitute a compositional unit except in the Psalms. It is well to remember that the chapter, paragraph, and verse divisions are purely editorial for the sake of convenience and are not found in the oldest manuscripts. However, a paragraph in the NASB, in general, is a unit of thought and very often two, three, or more paragraphs are grouped together as a unit by some idea, topic, or event. For the best results, a study unit should consist of not more than three or four paragraphs.

THE STUDY TOOLS

The following tools are a must:

• Bible (more than one translation)

- Pencil, colored pencils, paper
- Unabridged English dictionary
- Bible dictionary
- Bible commentaries.

THE STUDY METHOD

There are various methods to study the Bible. Each method, without question, has its own merit. However, the method adopted here is called the "analytical-synthetic method" (inductive Bible study). As the term suggests, this method begins with a detailed analysis of the passage with the intent to discover what the author actually wrote, and then continues with a *synthesis* of the parts to determine the message that the author is conveying. There are at least two important reasons for using this method.

- *It is objective in its approach.* It demands that one must first examine the details of the passage before drawing any conclusions.

- *It is impartial in its conclusion.* It demands that one's conclusion must be based on the facts (or evidence) discovered within the passage.

SUGGESTED PROCEDURE

There is no set pattern or procedure in this study method. Each individual should develop the kind of procedure that is best suited to him. However, one needs to be reminded that whatever study procedure one develops, it must be characterized by order, logic, and thoroughness. The following suggested steps serve as a guideline. (For those desiring to do a more exhaustive Bible study, consult *Methodical Bible Study: A New Approach to Hermeneutics* by Robert A. Traina.)

BECOME ACQUAINTED WITH THE PASSAGE

Read the passage over and over again until you are thoroughly familiar with its content.

RECOGNIZE THE LITERARY FORM OF THE PASSAGE

It is essential that you recognize the literary form of the passage at the outset. As you know, there is a variety of literary types represented in the Scriptures. Therefore, recognizing the literary form is a prerequisite to understanding the message of the passage. To quote Howard T. Kuist, "Form is the key which unlocks the door of content and discloses the essence of subject matter."[1] Generally, you will find the following literary forms in Scripture:

- *Historical narrative*—the gospels, Acts, Genesis, Joshua, Samuel
- *Discourse literature*—discourses of Jesus, epistles, and sermons
- *Parabolic literature*—the parables of Jesus
- *Poetic literature*—the Psalms, the Song of Solomon
- *Apocalyptic literature*—Revelation, parts of Daniel.

Keep in mind that, occasionally, you will find that various types of literature are combined together in a passage. In that case, literary form cannot be easily determined until the whole passage has been examined.

ANALYZE THE PASSAGE

According to Webster, to analyze "is to separate or break up (any whole) into its parts so as to find out their nature, proposition, function, and relationship." One of the best ways to analyze is to diagram the passage. Diagraming the passage has many advantages.

1. It enables you to see the passage as a whole and its grammatical structure.

2. It enables you to see not only what is said but how it is said.

3. It enables you to see the progression (or digression) of thought or events.

4. It enables you to see things that normally you would have missed.

In diagraming you must follow the text closely, proceeding from paragraph to paragraph. Since it is a recast of the text, you must copy word for word (use the NASB). *Never paraphrase it!* Read the following instructions carefully.

1. Take a sheet of paper and write the Scripture reference of the passage at the top.

2. Read a sentence at a time and identify the core

(a core consists of the main subject, verb, and object). Copy the core at the left side of the paper preceded by the reference.

3. Place the rest of the sentence, such as modified phrases and clauses, under the words or characters they describe.

4. Always place the connectives, such as conjunctions, by themselves in capital letters, so they may stand out.

5. Organize your diagram in such a way that when it is complete, the main ideas are all lined up.

6. Go over the diagram. Use graphic aids, such as underlining, arrows, circling, and boxing with colored pencils to indicate repetition, contrast, or comparison.

OBSERVE THE PASSAGE AND RAISE INTERPRETIVE QUESTIONS

According to Kuist, observation is "the art of seeing things as they really are." It entails seeing "impartially, intensely and fearlessly."[2] The importance of observation cannot be overemphasized because it is basic to understanding. One cannot understand what the given passage means unless one knows what the passage says. Charles R. Eberhardt rightly points out, "The aim of interpretation is re-creation of the author's intentions, and the first requirement, if this goal is to be achieved, is absolute mastery of the *form* and *content* of the record or composition" (italics added) .³ The mastery of content is possible only through minute observation, and this requires time and discipline. Again, read the following instructions carefully.

Observe the passage.

1. Use another sheet of paper and divide it into two columns. On the left hand column write "Observation" and on the right "Interpretive Question."

2. It is very important that you observe the passage as if you are seeing it for the first time.

3. Observation must begin with a clause as a whole, move to its various parts, and then its particulars.

4. Observation, in a sense, is "facts-hunting." Things you are to look for can be classified as follows:

   a. Pertaining to basic information—

   - Who?—characters

   - What?—events, sayings

   - When?—time

   - Where?—geographical location

   - How?—means.

   b. Pertaining to grammar—

   - Verb—tense? mood?

   - Pronoun—which person? singular or plural?

   - Conjunction?

   c. Pertaining to compositional features—

   • Repetition?

   • Comparison?

   • Contrast?

   • Progression or digression?

   • Cause and effect?

   • Question and answer?

   d. Others—

   • Atmosphere?

   • Illustration?

   • Idiomatic expression?

   • Figures of speech?

5. The best way to observe is by asking yourself questions like those listed above. That, of course, does not imply that the preceding list of questions is exhaustive, nor does it suggest that all the questions are applicable to every given passage indiscriminately. You must take the nature of the passage into consideration and exercise your own judgment.

6. Record your observations in the left-hand column of the paper. Always indicate the references. In regard to recording, two things need to be mentioned at this point. First, you should only record observations that are noteworthy rather than ev-

ery particular of the passage. Second, you should learn to organize your observations in such a way that they will be meaningful and useful to you in the future.

Ask interpretive questions.

1. As you proceed in observation, it is inevitable that you will raise many questions concerning the things you have observed—questions pertaining to meaning, reason, relationship, and implication. Those are questions for understanding, and are called "interpretive questions."

2. If your observation does not trigger questions in your mind, then you should learn to ask yourself questions. In fact, asking yourself questions will increase your power of concentration and will also make you think seriously about the meaning and implication of words, phrases, and clauses of the passage.

3. Learn to ask significant questions that will help to unlock the meaning of the words or sentences, and eventually the meaning of the passage. Bear in mind that observation and the raising of interpretive questions are not an end in themselves, but rather a means to an end; namely, to determine the message of the passage and to discover the intent of the author.

4. Record all the interpretive questions you asked

yourself in the right-hand column of the paper corresponding to the particular observation on which the questions were raised. Those questions are significant, for they function as a bridge between observation and interpretation.

5. Do not attempt to answer interpretive questions while you are doing observation. Learn to distinguish observation, interpretation, and application. Discipline yourself to do one thing at a time.

6. Try to classify the questions. It will help you to see in which areas they need clarification. You will notice that those questions generally fall into the following categories:

   • Definitive—pertaining to meaning

   • Rational—pertaining to reason

   • Structural—pertaining to relationship

   • Implicational—pertaining to things implied

   • Theological—pertaining to doctrine

   • Historical and Cultural—pertaining to background information.

7. Remember that the questions you raised vary in importance. Some questions may overlap and others may be found to be unanswerable. In general, the following kinds of questions should be omitted:

   • Questions that will lead to speculation

• Questions that are legitimate in themselves,
but are not relevant to the passage under
study.

INTERPRET THE PASSAGE: ANSWER THE INTERPRETIVE
   QUESTIONS

After you have completed a minute observation of
the passage, you are ready to make the transition to the
interpretative stage of your study. Interpretation that
logically follows observation is an attempt to discover
meaning the author intended to convey.

It is natural that your concerns, at this point, should
be how and where to find answers to the interpretive
questions that arose out of the observation. However,
you need to be reminded again that to answer those
questions is not an end in itself. Rather, it should be
a means whereby you may gain deeper insight into the
meaning of the whole passage.

The following factors and principles must be observed and conscientiously applied, if you are to interpret the author's words correctly and understand his
message accurately.

Subjective factors.

1. Spiritual sensitivity—In the interpretation, the
   divine illumination and one's spiritual sensitivity
   are closely related. The indwelling and illumination of the Holy Spirit are essential to spiritual
   understanding. Yet the degree of spiritual under-

standing depends upon one's spiritual sensitivity. Spiritual insensitivity is one of the obstacles to spiritual insight. It is only when that obstruction is removed that one can see and perceive. For that reason, preparation by prayer is an absolute necessity in the interpretation of the Scriptures. You must be willing to take time to pray and to meditate. In childlike humility, with a receptive heart, pray and trust the Holy Spirit for the following:

- To open your eyes and give spiritual insight (Luke 24:31)

- To open your mind to understand the Scriptures (Luke 24:45)

- To open the Scriptures to you (Luke 24:32).

2. Intellectual honesty—One must remember that interpretation is *ex*-egesis and not *eis*-egesis. Exegesis is approaching the passage with no preconceived notions of what it might mean or ought to mean, and bringing out the meaning that is native to the text. In other words, one must not read into the text (eisegesis) what it was never intended to mean. In the light of that, it is necessary that one should honestly examine his presuppositions and preconceptions before the interpretation. It is only with an open and unbiased mind that one can be true to the intent of the author.

Objective principles.

1. Consider the author's purpose—Interpret the passage in the light of the author's purpose and plan.

   Suggestion:

   To discover the purpose of a book is not always easy, since the majority of biblical writers did not state explicitly the purpose of their writings. However, a survey of the book (consult chapter 3, "A Survey of a Book") plus a careful study of its plan (or structure) should enable one to grasp the author's intention. Also, you may find this information in the introduction to the book in a Bible dictionary or commentary.

2. Consider the context of the passage—A passage must be interpreted in the light of its immediate and remote contexts. The importance of contextual interpretation is evident in the oft-quoted axiom, "A text without a context is only a pretext."

   Suggestion:

   The context of a passage will be more easily identified if one is familiar with the overall content of the book. Review the outline of the book.

3. Consider the literary form—In the interpretation, one must recognize the literary form of the

passage (including figures of speech) and interpret it accordingly.

Suggestion:

Books on biblical interpretation are an essential tool. Study "special hermeneutics."

4. Consider the historical-cultural setting—A passage must be understood in the light of the historical, cultural, social, political, and geographical setting in which it was composed. It is inevitable that all those factors had their influences on the writings.

Suggestion:

Good Bible commentaries, Bible dictionaries, a good Bible handbook, and a Bible history atlas are valuable sources of information.

5. Consider cumulative revelation—Since truth is many-sided, one must consider the total teaching of Scripture on the particular subject being interpreted. In other words, one must avoid drawing a final conclusion based on an *isolated text* (whether a verse or a passage), lest it result in extreme or one-sided views.

Suggestion:

Familiarize yourself with the Bible itself. Topical Bible references and cross-references are very helpful.

6. Compare Scripture with Scripture—Let the Bible be its own interpreter. Always interpret an obscure passage in the light of a clear one and not vice versa. Since divine revelation is self-consistent, one passage may shed light on another.

Suggestion:

Cross-references and a concordance are very helpful in this regard.

7. Seek the author's own interpretation—Look for Scripture's own interpretation. In the four gospels, Jesus and the writers often interpret their own words.

8. Follow the literal meaning—Take the words literally unless the context indicates otherwise. Remember that the Bible is much more frequently literal than figurative. Do not look for hidden meanings. Follow the advice, "If the literal sense makes good sense, seek no other sense, lest it result in nonsense."

Suggestion:

Generally speaking, one's common sense with the help of the context should be able to tell him whether the word is to be taken literally or figuratively.

9. Study the key words—The key words are impor-

tant clues to the message of the passage. In studying a word follow these steps:

a. Find its various meanings, including the root meaning, in an unabridged English dictionary or lexicon.

b. Tentatively decide on the meaning that best fits the context in which the word is found. Always relate that chosen meaning to the text itself and see whether it gives insight into the passage.

c. Investigate how this word is used in other passages, especially by the same author. Study also the parallel passage. Use a concordance.

d. Finally, determine the meaning of the word.

Suggestion:

An unabridged English dictionary, a lexicon, a concordance, and books on word study are invaluable tools. Also compare and contrast various translations which give different shades of meaning.

10. Consult commentaries—In the interpretation, outside aids such as commentaries are both desirable and necessary. In fact, they are invaluable tools if used at the proper time. One must avoid the pitfall that C. H. Spurgeon aptly observed. He said, "Two opposite errors beset the student of Scripture, the tendency to take every-

thing second hand from others, and the refusal to take anything from others." He is also reported to have said, "It seems odd that certain men who talk so much of what the Holy Spirit reveals to them should think so little of what He reveals to others." Remember commentaries are a tool—not a crutch!

Points to be considered.

1. The principles listed above are by no means exhaustive. Since biblical interpretation is such an important subject, one should make an effort to study this subject further.

2. Not all these principles must be taken into consideration in the interpretation of every passage. The nature of the passage being interpreted should dictate which principles are to be employed.

3. Even though these principles are individually listed, one will discover that some of them are interrelated.

4. It is not to be assumed that, even when one follows all of these study procedures, he will necessarily find the answer to all his questions or that he will always arrive, with certainty, at the meaning of the passage.

5. In regard to interpretive questions, do not try to answer each one of them. Use your own judg-

ment to select the kind of questions that, when answered, will give you insight into the message of the author.

6. Record the answers and interpretations on another sheet of paper. Leave enough space for additional notes later.

SYNTHESIZE THE PASSAGE AND SUMMARIZE ITS MESSAGE

One real danger in a detailed study, as discussed above, is that one might fail to see the forest for the trees. There is danger of getting lost in details and never coming to grasp the message of the passage as a whole. For that reason, it is both necessary and logical that synthesis and summary follow interpretation and precede application.

Synthesize the passage. Synthesis, the opposite of analysis, is "to put together parts or elements so as to form a whole" (Webster). In order to avoid the aforesaid danger two things are necessary: First, you must always consider the passage as a whole, remembering that the detailed analysis, minute observation, and careful interpretation are but a means to an end—to understand the message of the passage. Second, you must develop the ability to combine and to integrate your findings into a whole. Consider the following steps:

1. Determine the central teaching of the passage. Make it a habit always, at the end of Bible study, to ask yourself, "Why did the author select this

particular portion of material?" "What message did he try to communicate?" or "What would have been missed if this passage had been omitted?" With those questions in mind, go over your analysis of the passage carefully. Determine what you think to be the central message, and state it in your own words in a full sentence. The statement must be definite, precise, and accurate to the intent of the author.

2. Gather the supporting points. Try your best to form the habit of thinking by points. This will help you to think clearly and logically. Go over the analysis of the passage again. Gather the facts (details) that bear upon the central teaching, then organize these facts into supporting points and list them in a logical sequence. Perhaps the best way to do that is to study the structure of the passage carefully and take note of how the author arranged his material; how he developed his thought and accomplished his aim.

Summarize the message. To summarize is to present the teaching of the passage in a brief form. That can be done in various ways. For the sake of space, only the outline form will be discussed here.

1. Outline—A summary by means of outline is highly recommended because it shows in skeleton form the major teachings of the passage. There are two types of outlines:

    a. Topical—In this outline each point listed is directly related to one topic. All the points are more or less parallel in nature.

    b. Logical—In this outline the points are listed in natural logical sequence in which one point leads to another.

2. Headings—The heading for each point should be brief, suggestive, and easy to remember. The headings may be:

    a. Descriptive—This type of statement is more or less based on observation. The words are often taken from the text itself.

    b. Interpretive—This type of statement is interpretive in nature. It is based on the interpretation of the text.

3. Construction—The literary construction of the headings should be parallel.

Remember, a good summary should also reveal both the content and the structure of the passage.

MEDITATE UPON PERSONAL APPLICATION

One of the most common failures in much of Bible study is found at this point—the lack of emphasis on personal application. It has already been pointed out that the Bible was not given primarily for our information, but for our transformation. It is not just for studying; it is for living. So keep in mind that the final purpose of Bible study is not the acquisition of Bible knowledge, but the application of that knowledge. Observe the following steps in the process of application:

Assess the relevancy of the passage. Since each individual Bible passage varies in the degree of pertinence, it is necessary that you decide when, where, and for whom this particular passage is applicable.

Distinguish the timeless universal principle from the local practice. The principle may be stated explicitly or only implied in the text. The knowledge of the historical situation of the passage is essential in this regard.

Meditate over the newly discovered principle (or truth) until it becomes a personal conviction.

Think through thoroughly the personal application. Determine the area(s) of your life in which the principle is relevant.

Make one specific resolution. Concentrate on one application at a time.

Pray for the transforming power of the Holy Spirit to bring about the change needed in your life.

Keep a record of your personal application. For the details consult chapter 2, "Ezra, Our Model."

In summary, a proper, sound Bible study demands the involvement of the total person: mind, heart, and will. Truth requires not only an intellectual assent to its teaching, but also an obedient response to its message. It is required that the truth objectively perceived must be subjectively applied. Remember, as someone has aptly pointed out, light obeyed increases light, but light rejected brings night.

NOTES

1. Howard T. Kuist, *These Words Upon Thy Heart* (Richmond, Va.: John Knox, 1947), p. 92.
2. Ibid., p. 79 (John Ruskin as cited in Kuist).
3. Charles R. Eberhardt, *The Bible in the Making of Ministers* (New York: Association, 1949), p. 184.

5

HOW TO LEAD A GROUP BIBLE STUDY-DISCUSSION

What a Group Bible Study-Discussion Is

Group Bible study-discussion means exactly what the expression implies—a group of believers meet regularly to study the Bible by means of discussion. In order to avoid the misuse of the term, three things need special attention and elaboration.

IT IS A GROUP-DISCUSSION

Group Bible study-discussion stresses the importance of the participation of each member in the study-learning process. In other words, group Bible study-discussion allows no "spectator" or "audience" as in the case of a lecture. Every member, including the leader, is a participant and has the responsibility to bring helpful contributions to the group discussion.

IT EMPHASIZES STUDY

If the group discussion is to be effective for true learning to take place, the discussion must be accompanied by study. Facts must be examined, meanings must be studied, and the truth discovered. Without such preparation and information, discussion is likely to degenerate into an "opinion-exchange" or even into a "group therapy."

IT FOCUSES ON THE BIBLE

If the group Bible study-discussion would be true to its name, the Bible must occupy the central place. The group needs to be constantly reminded that its task is to study the Bible, and not books about the Bible or church doctrine. The discussion must be centered on the biblical text of the day. The group must guard against the danger of going off on a tangent or turning the meeting into a social visit.

The Purpose and the Goal of Group Bible Study-Discussion

The group members must know that the purpose of Bible study is not only to discover what the Bible says, but to understand what God is saying to each member through the passage studied. That is, Bible study does not and must not stop at the *acquisition* of knowledge; it must go beyond to the *application* of that knowledge. That means that each member must come to grips with these two questions: What is God speaking to *me* here and now through this study? and How am *I* to translate it into experience and action? Each individual must be willing, if the study is to be effective, to search his or her own heart honestly for the answers and share them with the group. Obviously, the goal of group Bible study-discussion is to help its members to learn and to grow in Christian knowledge and experience; to let the Word of God shape the life of each individual so that that individual may develop Christlike character.

THE RESPONSIBILITY OF GROUP MEMBERS

Since group Bible study-discussion depends very much on its members, the responsibilities of each member must be clearly explained at the outset. The members must come to see that the quality and the outcome of the group study are determined by the following factors.

PRESENCE

The importance of attending the meeting regularly by the group members hardly needs any comment. Obviously, no group is worth meeting if its members drop in at their convenience or only when they happen to have nothing more interesting to do.

PREPARATION

A faithful preparation of the assignment before the meeting by each member is something that cannot be overemphasized. If the group is to experience "in-depth" Bible study, the members must bring the rich resources of careful preparation to the study-discussion. In other words, the quality of the meeting is in proportion to the amount of study and thinking that the members of the group give to its lesson before the meeting.

PARTICIPATION

Since it is learning together as a group, active participation in discussion by each member must be emphasized. In fact, the give-and-take of the learning process brings both interest and satisfaction to those who participate. Generally, those who have studied before the meeting are likely to participate because they have something to contribute to the group.

PRACTICE

The members of the group need to be constantly reminded that the heart of the matter is personal, and the goal of the Bible study is practical. Each member has the responsibility to *translate* the acquired knowledge into action.

PRAYER

Since group Bible study-discussion is a corporate searching for the message of God, for the group as well as for the individual, the members of the group must be willing to pray for one another so that the purpose of the group and the goal of each individual may be realized.

THE QUALIFICATIONS OF THE GROUP LEADER

It is true that the success of group Bible study-discussion depends on its members. But, it is equally true that much depends on the leader of the group. A group leader should have the following qualifications:

BE A GROWING CHRISTIAN

A good leader must:

Love to study the Word of God

Experience the Lordship of Christ in his or her daily life

Understand the work and the leading of the Holy Spirit

Know the secret and the power of prayer.

HAVE A WELL-ROUNDED PERSONALITY

A good leader is:

Genuine and sincere. A group leader does not pretend to be someone else, but says what he or she means.

Emotionally stable. Such a leader must not be irritable nor easily offended. He should never be defensive but face criticism honestly and objectively.

Intellectually honest. Does not hesitate to acknowledge personal limitations. A leader should be quick to learn from others and allow others to disagree with him.

Friendly. A leader accepts others as they are. He or she makes every member feel at home and that each has worthwhile contributions to make to the group study-discussion.

A good listener. A leader must be skilled in listening as well as in speaking. He must have the ability to get others to think and talk, to contribute, and to learn from active participation in the group.

Tactful in dealing with people. A leader must be able to handle even difficult situations without embarrassing the participants.

IS A RESPONSIBLE PERSON

A good leader:

Takes his commitment seriously.

Prepares work faithfully and prays for the group regularly.

Tries to improve skills, to increase his or her knowledge, and to understand the group members.

Evaluates personal performance honestly.

Is not self-seeking, but willing to take the role of a servant.

THE ROLE OF GROUP LEADER

It will help to define what the role of a group leader is by stating first what a leader is not:

1. The group leader is not a "teacher." The relationship between the leader and the group is not one of "teacher-student" relationship; the teacher

who has answers and the student who has questions.

2. The group leader is not a "lecturer." Again the leader's relationship to the group is not a "lecturer-audience" relationship; one who does all the talking and the group listening.

THE LEADER AS A HELPER-GUIDE

Then, what role does the leader play? A leader's role is simply a "helper-guide." Though maybe not so obvious, the role of a helper-guide is a significant one because of its primary tasks, which are:

1. *To motivate the group to study*—Make the study relevant and discussion interesting, and help the members to set personal goals as motivating factor for study.

2. *To stimulate the group to think*—Help the members to do their own thinking and to discover the truth for themselves.

3. *To guide the group in study-discussion*—Keep the discussion going and guide it in the general direction of the planned goals or objectives.

4. *To encourage the group to participate*—Help the members learn to express themselves and to interact with one another.

5. *To challenge the group to put into practice*—Suggest ways or opportunities for personal response or application.

An effective group leader must first come to see the significance of such group study and then seek to understand how to provide opportunities for the purposeful participation of the members. However, a leader must be constantly on his guard as the danger to dominate the discussion is always there. And the temptation to parade knowledge always lurks at the corner. It will help if the leader would keep in mind that people learn best when they work at it; when they do their own study and thinking.

How a Leader Plans for a Group Bible Study-Discussion

As far as meeting-place, time, size of group, or frequency of meeting are concerned, there is no rigid rule. They must be determined by the members of the group both by reason and prayer. However, the following suggestions may serve as guidelines.

MEETING-PLACE

The physical setting must be conducive to learning. Generally, the meeting-place should be as attractive and comfortable as possible. A home setting is an ideal meeting-place, because it provides an informal, relaxing atmosphere.

TIME

For the best results, a meeting lasts an hour or an hour and a half at the most. Remember, discussion beyond this point usually brings no benefit.

SIZE OF THE GROUP

The ideal number of group members is probably somewhere between seven and ten. That is small enough to have the much-desired openness, honesty, and personal interaction. At the same time, it is large enough to have the diversity of background.

FREQUENCY OF MEETING

Weekly meetings are highly recommended. That provides enough time for preparation, and yet not too long as to lose the continuity of thought and eventually the loss of interest.

NUMBER OF MEETINGS

They could be scheduled for a short term or a long term according to the desire and the convenience of the group members. For a short term, the group should begin meeting right after Labor Day and end before Christmas, or begin in January and end in May. For a long term, meetings generally begin in September and last until May, the following year.

STUDY MATERIALS

It is very important for the members to take part in selecting the topics for study. They are likely to be more interested than when study materials are chosen by others. Whatever the decision may be, the group members need to know the portions of materials to be studied week by week.

How a Leader Prepares for a Study Session

BEGIN WITH PERSONAL STUDY

A group leader needs to remember that unless he or she masters the passage and comes to grips with its message, he cannot prepare the lesson intelligently or lead the group study effectively. While studying, the leader must follow "The Law of the Spirit" (consult chapter 1, "Study the Bible with Both Heart and Mind") and cover the following steps:

a. Look for the relation of the passage to its context.

b. Seek to understand the passage in its original setting.

c. Try to visualize the scene and the event.

d. Find the structure of the passage.

e. Observe the significant facts of the passage.

f. Study the meanings of the words or phrases.

g. Look up the references or parallel passages.

h. Read other translations for different shades of meaning.

i. Interpret the thoughts of the passage (consult outside aids).

j. Make comparisons with corresponding views or customs of the present days.

k. Find illustrations from one's own experiences.

l. Try to paraphrase the passage in modern language.

   m. Summarize the central teaching of the passage and make an outline.

   n. Draw principles or implications suggested in the text.

   o. Consider personal applications.

MAKE A GENERAL PLAN

After a thorough study of the passage, the leader should work out a general plan for the meeting by which he expects to guide the group in study-discussion. It does not mean that the plan must be rigidly carried out. However, a general plan gives the leader both the direction and the confidence needed to lead the discussion. If the leader has no plan, he will be left without resources when things do not go well, will feel lost, and will possibly even feel a sense of failure at the end. The plan should include:

Aim. Every study-discussion should have an aim that the leader keeps to himself. The leader will have a clear-cut aim if he answers these basic questions, "What do I want to accomplish through this lesson?" or "What should the group members learn and experience through this study?"

Introduction. An introduction is determined by the aim, the nature of the passage, and by the nature of the group as well. The leader should ask himself, "How do I get started so that it will create interest and secure the attention of the group?" The following are examples.

- Review the preceding lesson(s)
- Present a problem
- Introduce the historical-cultural background out of which the passage arose
- Brief survey of the passage
- Present an outline of the passage
- Use visual aids

Content. It is obvious that not every statement found in the passage has equal significance and value in the light of the chosen aim. In order to accomplish the objective in mind, the leader should ask himself, "What portion of the text do I select for emphasis?" "What is the outline of the lesson?"

Conclusion. The leader should ask himself, "How would I conclude this lesson?" "In what specific way can I make this study personal?" "How do I challenge the members to put it into action?"

Method. Generally, group study-discussion is one of the best methods of learning, for it offers greater opportunity for participation by its members. However, there are several other possible variations of the discussion method which the leader should try occasionally in order to maintain interest in the group and to avoid monotony. At each preparation, the leader should ask, "What is the most appropriate method for studying this particular passage by this particular group to achieve a particular objective?"

PREPARE A WEEKLY STUDY-DISCUSSION GUIDE

It is highly recommended that the leader prepare a weekly study guide for the group members, for that will help in their own preparation and also in group discussion. The study guide should include at least two things:

Background information. The leader should indicate the source where such information could be obtained, if it is needed to make the understanding of the passage intelligent.

Thought-provoking questions. The leader uses the outline of the passage to be studied as a framework to prepare questions for the group to think about before they come to the meeting. Those questions serve both as a guide in personal preparation and a catalyst in group study-discussion. But the leader must emphasize that each member does his own study of the passage first before using the questionnaire.

How a Leader Prepares a Questionnaire

FUNCTION OF QUESTIONS

The method of questioning, by no means, is the only method to study the Bible, but it is an effective method. A good question has at least the following functions:

• It creates interest and secures attention.

- It stimulates the thinking and sets the mind to work.

- It directs attention to a new thought and helps to gain insight.

- It helps create a learning experience.

- It generates good discussion.

TYPES OF QUESTIONS

Generally, there are three basic types of questions:

Questions of information. Questions that help to observe significant facts.

Questions of interpretation. Questions that help to unlock the meaning of the author and that open doors to new insights.

Questions of application. Questions that make one think about personal application and challenge one to put it into action.

TESTS FOR GOOD QUESTIONS

Unless the group chooses to use a study course, the leader should prepare a questionnaire. But he soon will discover that to frame questions skillfully is not an easy job, it requires much practice. However, use the following tests as guidelines in the formation of questions:

- Is the question clear and easy to understand?

- Does it give enough information to guide the thinking?

- Does it have a definite answer, or will it lead to speculation?

- Does it stimulate the thought processes?

- Does it make a point worth discussing at this time by this group?

- Does the question reveal the answer?

- Is the sequence of the questions geared to the continuity of the event or the thought of the passage? Does it direct toward the aim of the lesson?

Probably, the best way to test a questionnaire is for the leader to try to answer it himself. Questions that are too vague or too involved; questions that can be answered by "Yes" or "No"; and questions whose answers are self-evident have no value and should be omitted.

How a Leader Leads a Group Bible Study-Discussion

GROUND RULES FOR GROUP MEMBERS

Certain basic principles govern the quality of study-discussion groups. Those principles must be followed if the group members desire to have an effective study-discussion group meeting where true learning actually takes place.

1. The group members must realize that little can be accomplished unless the entire group cooperates actively.

2. The group members must help to create a relaxing atmosphere of understanding and acceptance where each member feels free to participate and to express himself. Each member must be himself and accept others as they are.

3. Each member should be attentive. Listen carefully to what others say and try to understand their points of view.

4. Each member must be willing not only to learn from others, but also to subject his or her ideas to the judgment of the group.

5. Each member must be considerate of the others, for example:

   • No one should monopolize the discussion in such a way that it gives no chance for others to talk or to react.

   • No one should insist upon his or her own viewpoint and refuse to consider that of anyone else.

   • No one should be argumentative or critical (in a negative way) in discussing conflicts of opinion.

6. Each member should genuinely be concerned for one another and minister to one another's needs.

PRACTICAL SUGGESTIONS FOR THE GROUP LEADER

Business matters.

1. In a study-discussion meeting, the members, including the leader, should seat themselves informally in a circle or around a table so that they can see each other. Leave a few chairs near the door for the occasional latecomers.

2. The leader should know the individual members by name and make sure that the members of the group get acquainted with each other.

3. The leader should begin each meeting promptly and close on time. Never wait for those who are late or drag the meeting on beyond the prearranged time.

Study-discussion procedure.

1. Prayer—The meeting must begin with prayer seeking the illumination of the Spirit and proceed with an expectancy that God will speak to the group through the study-discussion. (Remember "The Law of the Spirit," chapter 1).

2. Reading—It is wise to ask the group to read the passage to be discussed in silence or have one member read it for the group. This will help them to gather their wandering thoughts and focus their attention on the passage.

3. Introduction—This can be done by the leader or by a member arranged ahead of time.

4. Questions from the members—It is highly recommended that the leader prepare a chalkboard and write on it a logical division of the passage with references. Before the discussion gets underway, give the group an opportunity to raise questions that the passage might suggest to their mind and that they would like to be discussed. Have a member assist by writing the questions on the chalkboard under the appropriate divisions. The leader incorporates those into the questionnaire he has previously prepared.

5. Study-discussion—Use paragraphs as basic units of discussion, and examine each verse carefully. Here are some tips for leading a discussion:

   a. Pertaining to questions

      • Remember that the questionnaire is meant to be a guide and not to be followed slavishly. Be flexible and skip any questions that do not fit into the flow of discussion as it progresses.

      • Make sure that the questions raised by the members are discussed.

      • Never answer your own question. Don't be afraid of silence! If necessary, rephrase the question and ask again.

- Always direct questions to the group as a whole first, then to a particular member in the group.

b. Pertaining to discussion

- Make sure that the discussion is carried on in an informal atmosphere of friendliness and openness, so that no one feels hesitant to participate in discussion or to ask questions.

- Exercise care to keep the discussion centered on the passage and avoid going off on a tangent no matter how interesting the direction.

- Be sure to keep the entire scope and aim of the lesson well in view and keep discussion moving from one important point to another. Don't let discussion become bogged down by minor points or nonessentials.

- Be sure to spend enough time in discussing the meaning of the text (interpretation) and the meaning of the passage for today (relevancy), so that the group finds itself discussing real issues in the lives of its members.

- Don't be satisfied with the first answer, especially when it comes to interpretation.

Encourage interaction and comments on one another's answers and ideas.

• If someone should ask a question during the discussion, do not try to answer it. Turn the question to the group for answer first.

• Receive all contributions warmly regardless of its merit. In case of a wrong answer, don't correct it bluntly. Ask the group to comment on it. Be sure to avoid embarrassing the participant.

• Be sure to give each member a chance to participate. Tactfully hold in check those who tend to monopolize the discussion and draw out those who are more inhibited.

c. Pertaining to the leader

• As a leader, try to know the strengths and weaknesses; the special interests and problems of each member.

• As a leader, give the members self-confidence and a sense of security to express themselves.

• As a leader, don't talk too much! Express your own views as a member of the group.

• As a leader, always be ready to help the group to distinguish between fact and opinion; to clarify the differences of viewpoints in case of controversial issues; to bring out the main issues in discussion; and to summarize the conclusion as it is needed.

6. Conclusion—It is the responsibility of the leader to close the meeting on time. Never allow the discussion to drag on so that the members leave one by one. Be conscious of time! The leader must see to it that enough time is spared for the following:

a. Be sure to summarize the main teachings of the passage in an outline form at the end of the discussion. Have a member assist by writing them on the chalkboard.

b. Be sure to spend time sharing personal applications and what the members of the group learn through the study.

c. Be sure to close the meeting with a period of prayer. Make a genuine effort to make the group Bible study-discussion a "study-fellowship-prayer group."

OUR MODEL: BEREAN BIBLE STUDY GROUP

"For they received the word with great eagerness, examining the Scriptures daily, to see whether these things were so. Many of them therefore believed" (Acts 17:11).

RECEIVED	—implies *openness, readiness* • Without reception, the words would have fallen on rocky ground.
WITH . . . EAGERNESS	—implies *keen desire, enthusiasm, alertness, attention* • These are fundamental factors which promote effective learning.
EXAMINING	—implies an *inquisitive, active mind* • It means to investigate, to scrutinize. • To examine means "to look into critically or methodically in order to find out the facts."
EXAMINING THE SCRIPTURE	—implies the *final authority of the Scripture* • Man's word must be tested by the the Word of God. We must bring the message of the preacher or the word of the teacher under the scrutiny of the Word of God
EXAMINING . . . DAILY	—implies *diligence, persistence, effort* • Remember the essential ingredients to success in life are clear-cut goals, determination, effort, sacrifice, and persistence.
EXAMINING . . . TO SEE WHETHER THESE THINGS WERE SO	—implies *caution* • Genuine faith must be built on the Word of God, and not on the word of man (John 4:41).

BIBLIOGRAPHY

Adler, Mortimer J. *How to Read a Book*. Rev. ed. New York: Simon & Schuster, 1972.

Barclay, William. *Introducing the Bible*. Nashville: Abingdon, 1972.

Berkhof, Louis. *Principles of Biblical Interpretation*. Grand Rapids: Baker, 1950.

Dewey, John. *How to Think*. D. C. Heath and Co., 1910.

Eberhardt, C. R. *The Bible in the Making of Ministers*. New York: Association, 1949.

Gettys, J. M. *How to Enjoy Studying the Bible*. Richmond: John Knox, 1950.

———. *How to Teach the Bible*. Richmond: John Knox, 1950.

Gregory, J. M. *The Seven Laws of Learning*. Rev. ed. Grand Rapids: Baker, 1955.

Jensen, Irving L. *Enjoy Your Bible*. Chicago: Moody, 1969.

———. *Independent Bible Study*. Chicago: Moody, 1963.

Job, John B., ed. *How to Study the Bible*. Downers Grove, Ill.: Inter-Varsity, 1974.

Kuist, H. T. *These Words Upon Thy Heart*. Richmond: John Knox, 1947.

Little, Sara. *Learning Together in the Christian Fellowship*. Richmond: John Knox, 1962.

Mickelsen, A. Berkeley. *Interpreting the Bible*. Grand Rapids: Eerdmans, 1963.

Ramm, Bernard L. *Hermeneutics*. Grand Rapids: Baker, 1967.

Richardson, Alan. *A Preface to Bible Study*. Philadelphia: Westminster, 1944.

Sterrett, T. Norton. *How to Understand Your Bible*. Downers Grove, Ill.: Inter-Varsity, 1974.

Stibbs, Alan M. *Understanding God's Word*. London: The Inter-Varsity Fellowship, 1950.

Stott, John R. W. *Understanding the Bible*. Glendale, Calif.: Regal, Gospel Light, 1972.

Tenney, Merrill C. *New Testament Times*. Grand Rapids: Eerdmans, 1965.

Terry, Milton S. *Biblical Hermeneutics*. Grand Rapids: Zondervan, 1964.

Traina, Robert A. *Methodical Bible Study*. New York: Ganis & Harris, 1957.

Vos, Howard F. *Effective Bible Study.* Grand Rapids: Zondervan, 1956.

Wald, Oletta. *The Joy of Discovery.* Minneapolis: Augsburg, 1976.

NOTES

NOTES

NOTES

NOTES

NOTES

NOTES

NOTES

NOTES

NOTES

NOTES

NOTES